HISTORY OF
★ CIVIL RIGHTS ★
IN AMERICA

Eastern National promotes the public's understanding and support of
America's national parks and other public trust partners by providing
quality educational experiences, products, and services.

For more information, please contact Eastern National,
470 Maryland Drive, Fort Washington, PA 19034.
Visit us at www.eParks.com

Special thanks to National Park Service personnel
who helped in the production of this book.

ISBN 978-1-59091-150-1

Welcome from the Director

On behalf of the National Park Service, I am pleased to present this guide to one of the most compelling chapters of American history. The diverse park sites contained here tell part of the story. They include Little Bighorn Battlefield National Monument where it commemorates one of the American Indians' last armed efforts to preserve their way of life and engages the darker side of the American past; César E. Chávez National Monument, the home and workplace of César Chávez, whose courage, perseverance, and tenacity was a beacon of hope to the united farm workers movement; and the Selma to Montgomery National Historic Trail, which has earned iconic status as a symbol of the civil rights movement.

Woven together, they illustrate the continuum of the civil rights story in America. This concise guide offers a quick tour of this legacy, and while it is intended to make a vast and complicated subject accessible, it is also designed to encourage a closer look. Through this guide, we invite you to visit these national parks and monuments to explore the rich history that is available via the National Park Service's preservation of these places and the scholarly research that allows these stories to be told.

A century separates the firing on Fort Sumter from the Freedom Rides, but the ongoing struggle to build a truly unified nation in the war's wake connects the two eras through generations of continuing struggles for justice and equality for all. This notion confounds those who seek to separate the Civil War from the fundamental questions of slavery and citizenship, or who choose to remember the civil rights movement as a time when the country suddenly awoke from a 70-year slumber of disfranchisement and discrimination. The contrived and artificial separation between these two eras would seem strange both to those who fought Jim Crow and to those who rallied to save it.

The National Park Service has the privilege of being entrusted with this narrative, with preserving and interpreting its complexity and depth. We are the keeper of the American legacy in all its sweep and drama. At every turn of this narrative, there are important lessons for today. These places, these national parks, have been set aside for future generations, not because they are old, but because they are timeless in teaching American history.

—NPS Director Jonathan B. Jarvis

Telling the Story

We believe that National Park Service parks and programs offer the finest laboratories for understanding our history. Starting with Jamestown, the site of the first permanent English settlement in North America, to César E. Chávez National Monument—the headquarters for the farm labor movement in the late 20th century and one of the newest national parks—we share the stories of places in which rights and liberties were achieved, as well as the places where rights and liberties were denied.

To nearly every American, few concepts are more important than their rights and their liberties. But what exactly do these words mean? To some, the right to own a gun is one of their most important rights. To others, the right of governments to prohibit gun ownership is an important right.

Confusion over the meanings of these words is not new. One hundred fifty years ago, President Abraham Lincoln recognized this confusion in a speech he delivered in Baltimore in April 1864: "The world has never had a good definition of the word liberty," he said. "…the American people, just now, are much in want of one. We all declare for liberty; but in using the same word we do not all mean the same thing. With some the word liberty may mean for each man to do as he pleases with himself, and the product of his labor; while with others the same word may mean for some men to do as they please with other men, and the product of other men's labor. Here are two, not only different, but incompatible things, called by the same name—liberty."

On his inaugural journey to Washington, D.C., Abraham Lincoln spoke at Independence Hall in Philadelphia, Pennsylvania, on February 22, 1861 and raised the 35-star American flag. Print after a painting by Jean Leon Gerome Ferris, ca. 1908.

He continued: "The shepherd drives the wolf from the sheep's throat, for which the sheep thanks the shepherd as a liberator, while the wolf denounces him for the same act as the destroyer of liberty, especially as the sheep was a black one. Plainly the sheep and the wolf are not agreed upon a definition of the word liberty; and precisely the same difference prevails to-day among us human creatures, even in the North, and all professing to love liberty. Hence we behold the processes by which thousands are daily passing from under the yoke of bondage, hailed by some as the advance of liberty, and bewailed by others as the destruction of all liberty."

Establishing Jamestown

We in the 21st century have our concepts of rights and liberties. We believe—and our Constitution confirms—that all adult citizens over the age of 18 have the right to vote. There are quibbles over how people register to vote, what might be required to prove that they are registered, etc., but the basic concept is that all adult citizens can vote. In Jamestown, Virginia, established in 1607

The marriage of Pocahontas and John Rolfe at Jamestown, Virginia, in April 1614. Lithograph, 19th century.

(Jamestown National Historic Site), the governor of the colony was selected by the king. The governor appointed his council, and members of the House of Burgesses were elected. But the only Virginians eligible to vote were adult males who owned property or a few who rented substantial farms. Thus, the right to vote was limited to a very small minority, which was acceptable to the general population.

One significant difference between the Jamestown settlement and other early colonies was that early on, the native population lived pretty much in harmony with the white population. The 14,000 to 21,000 American Indians living in eastern Virginia at the time consisted of allied tribes, each with its own ruler, living in its own community. The Powhatan Confederacy, as it was called, had one supreme ruler who wielded ultimate authority over all the tribes and to whom each paid tribute. The concept here was that the Powhatan Confederacy had the rights to its own lands, and the white settlers had rights to their own lands. Colonist John Rolfe married the young Indian woman, Pocahontas, daughter of Wahunsenacawh, chief of the Powhatan Confederacy, which helped to seal the peaceful relations between settlers and natives. However, as more and more settlers came to Virginia, and after Wahunsenacawh died, the peaceful relationship deteriorated. Further, in Virginia and elsewhere, most new settlers decided that the Indians no longer had the right to their lands— creating conflicts that would last for over 250 years.

In 1619, at about the same time the peace between Virginia's settlers and natives was beginning to fracture, another event took place that would have repercussions for centuries to come. The *White Lion*, a British ship under a Dutch flag, landed near the mouth of Chesapeake Bay in need of repairs and supplies. On board were 20 African slaves which the Virginia settlers purchased, thus beginning the institution of slavery in what would later become the United States.

As the colonies were established and grew, the model established in Virginia continued. A governor, in most cases appointed by the king, was the executive. A legislative body—generally— was elected by property-owning adult males. Gradually, however, property requirements were relaxed in some colonies, allowing more men to vote. Also, American colonists had an unusually high literacy rate, and they read the newspapers that sprang up everywhere. Thus, they were well-informed about events and wanted to vote.

Emerging Causes

In 1733, John Peter Zenger, a German immigrant, started printing articles in his newspaper, *The New York Weekly Journal*, that were critical of New York Governor William Cosby. Because New Yorkers read Zenger's newspaper, opposition to Cosby grew, and a year later, Zenger was arrested for malicious libel. The charges were not that Zenger was printing lies, rather that he was critical of the governor. In 1735, in one of the most important trials in American history, Zenger's case came to trial, and he was defended by Philadelphian Andrew Hamilton, one of the finest lawyers in the colonies.

Hamilton first demanded that the case be tried before a jury—a right that Zenger could claim. Then the lawyer stated that Zenger had indeed written all he was accused of in his newspaper, but everything he wrote was true. Therefore, truth was the best defense against libel. He won his case, Zenger was acquitted, and one of the bedrock American principles of freedom of the press was established. These events are commemorated at Saint Paul's Church National Historic Site and Federal Hall National Memorial in New York.

Some historians have described British rule in the American colonies as "benign neglect." That's probably an overstatement, but American colonists enjoyed more rights and privileges than residents in England. So, after the conclusion of the French and Indian War (commemorated at Fort Necessity National Battlefield), as the British began an effort to recoup some of the expenses of fighting much of the war in North America, the colonists vigorously reacted and began to think of themselves as Americans as much as they saw themselves as New Yorkers, Pennsylvanians, etc. When the British Parliament passed the Stamp Act in 1765 as an effort to raise revenue, the colonists joined forces to condemn the act and to find ways to circumvent its impact.

A demonstration against the Stamp Act in New York City, November 1, 1765. Wood engraving, American, 1850.

Letters circulated throughout the colonies calling for a conference to be held in New York on the site presently occupied by Federal Hall National Memorial. The colonists were beginning to recognize that they had more in common with each other than they did with the British brothers and sisters. More importantly though, as part of the outcome of this Stamp Act Congress held in New York, the delegates drafted the Declaration of Rights and Grievances of the Colonies as a petition to the king for relief and as a petition to Parliament to repeal the Stamp Act. The main focus of this petition was that the rights of the colonists were denied. The colonies were being taxed without representation, which violated a bedrock principle of the British Constitution.

The Stamp Act and the other British actions designed to raise revenue and/or control colonial activities were disastrous, leading to the American Revolution. Beyond simply reading about the American Revolution, Americans can see and feel the places where many of these events took place in national park units. You can walk the 2.5-mile-long Freedom Trail in Boston National Historical Park and see Old South Meeting House, Old State House, Faneuil Hall, the Paul Revere House, and Old North Church which bring to life the American ideals of freedom of speech, religion, government, and self-determination. The trail also leads to Charlestown, where you can visit the Bunker Hill Monument, the site of the first major battle of the American Revolution.

"We hold these truths to be self-evident…"

In Philadelphia, you can visit Carpenters' Hall and Independence Hall, where the Continental Congress met, adopted the Declaration of Independence, the Articles of Confederation, and where several years later the Constitutional Convention adopted a new constitution. Also, at Independence National Historical Park, you can visit Franklin Court, the site of Benjamin Franklin's home, and Congress Hall, where both houses of Congress met from 1790 to 1800, and where they were meeting when the Bill of Rights was adopted. Another site, the reconstructed Graff House, was where Thomas Jefferson penned the Declaration of Independence in the summer of 1776, which began with the phrase, "We hold these truths to be self-evident, that all men are created equal."

What did this phrase mean? Clearly Jefferson did not mean that all men were created equal—in particular his slaves—nor did he include women in the equation. To Frederick Douglass, an African American man who had escaped from slavery and who became a powerful advocate for the antislavery movement, the Declaration of Independence was a sham. He asked in a speech in 1852: "Are the

Frederick Douglass

great principles of political freedom and of natural justice, embodied in that Declaration of Independence, extended to us [African Americans]?" He further asked: "What, to the American slave, is your 4th of July?" He answered that it is "a day that reveals to him, more than all other days in the year, the gross injustice and cruelty to which he is the constant victim. To him, your celebration is a sham; your boasted liberty, an unholy license; your national greatness, swelling vanity; your sounds of rejoicing are empty and heartless; your denunciations of tyrants, brass fronted impudence; your shouts of liberty and equality, hollow mockery; your prayers and hymns, your sermons and thanksgivings, with all your religious parade, and solemnity, are, to him, mere bombast, fraud, deception, impiety, and hypocrisy— a thin veil to cover up crimes which would disgrace a nation of savages. There is not a nation on the earth guilty of practices, more shocking and bloody, than are the people of these United States, at this very hour." Frederick Douglass National Historic Site commemorates the life of this great orator and tireless worker for equal rights for everyone.

So, the "all men are created equal" phrase related to white males, who in most cases owned property; it excluded enslaved people and women. But, even with these exclusions, the Declaration of Independence established a precedent that would become more inclusive later.

Jefferson based much of the Declaration of Independence, and particularly the preamble, on the recently adopted Virginia Declaration of Rights. A month or so before Jefferson put his pen to paper, George Mason had proposed an enumeration of rights to the Virginia Constitutional Convention, which became Article I of the Virginia Constitution. The 16 rights included freedom of the press, freedom of religion, protection from unlawful search or seizure, and so forth. The Declaration was the first instance in which individual rights were protected. Further, since they were incorporated in the Virginia Constitution, they could not be changed except by constitutional amendment.

In 1787, as the Constitutional Convention was concluding its work in Philadelphia, George Mason, a delegate from Virginia, recommended the incorporation of a "bill of rights" into the new constitution. He argued that it "would give great quiet to the people; and with the aid of the State declarations, a bill might be prepared in a few hours." His proposal was denied. To Americans at the

Signing the U.S. Constitution, 1787. Oil on canvas, 1940, by Howard Chandler Christy.

time—again, white males who generally owned property—the protection of their rights had become so important, the omission in the Constitution became a major stumbling block during the ratification debate that followed.

When Virginia's ratifying convention met in 1788, James Madison agreed that as soon as the legislature convened under the new constitution, one of the first orders of business would be to draft a bill of rights that would be submitted to the states as amendments to the Constitution. Madison kept his word and as a member of the House of Representatives introduced a bill of rights in 1789. Congress approved the amendments and submitted them to the states later that year. They were ratified in December 1791. Congress was meeting in the site of Federal Hall in New York to adopt the Bill of Rights, and Congress was meeting in Congress Hall in Philadelphia when they were adopted.

There were interesting nuances in the Bill of Rights. Americans were leery of a strong central government, so the first amendment, which enumerated freedom of religion, speech, the press, assembly, and the right to petition the government for a redress of grievances, began with "Congress shall make no law respecting...." In other words, these rights and liberties were the law of the land; they could not be altered except by constitutional amendment.

Enslaved people certainly did not enjoy the "blessings of liberty." But women did not enjoy many of these blessings either. On July 13, 1848, near Seneca Falls, about 300 miles from New York City, a well-to-do Quaker couple, Jane and Richard Hunt, hosted a tea party in their home. They invited their neighbor, Elizabeth Cady Stanton, as well as Mary Ann M'Clintock, wife of a Quaker minister, and Lucretia Mott and her sister Martha Coffin Wright. This must have been some tea party! The conversation centered on their discontent concerning their civil and legal status. They decided to take action on their grievances and called for a convention to be held one week later in Seneca Falls, with Lucretia Mott as the keynote speaker.

They posted a notice in the local newspaper for the meeting to be held July 19-20 in the Wesleyan Chapel in Seneca Falls to discuss the "social, civil, and religious condition of women." About 300 people attended, including Frederick Douglass, and at the end of the two-day convention, 100 of them signed the "Declaration of Sentiments," a document modeled after the Declaration of Independence, which made bold demands for its day.

Women's suffrage leaders Elizabeth Cady Stanton, Carrie Chapman Clinton Catt, and Lucretia Mott on a United States postage stamp, 1948.

American women should have civil and political rights equal to their male counterparts, including the right to vote. The Declaration is interpreted at Women's Rights National Historical Park.

Slavery: Catalyst for Civil War

It would take nearly a century before women gained the constitutional right to vote. But women in 1848 at least had the right to hold a convention and freely express their grievances. Enslaved Americans, on the other hand, had no such rights. In fact, they had no rights whatsoever.

With our 21st-century lens, it is very difficult for us to understand that on the eve of the Civil War, there were nearly four million enslaved human beings in the United States. It's equally hard for us to understand that viewing the institution of slavery as an evil was at the time something relatively new in human history. The Babylonian Code of Hammurabi, one of the oldest surviving codes of law, dating to about 1700 BC, includes several laws dealing with slavery. Granted, most enslaved people were not happy with their lot in life, but seldom, if ever, did the slave-owning class see anything wrong with slavery.

What was slavery like in the United States? Our national parks don't tell the whole story, but several of our parks open windows into the institution. Cane River Creole National Historical Park in Louisiana interprets plantation life. The site includes several quarters in which enslaved people lived. Hampton National Historic Site in Maryland; Arlington House, The Robert E. Lee Memorial in Virginia; and the Kingsley Plantation—part of Timucuan Ecological and Historic Preserve in Florida—interpret different aspects of plantation culture. Natchez National Historical Park in Mississippi interprets slavery at the Melrose Plantation, and also tells the story of nearby Forks of the Road, which was one of the largest slave markets in the South.

American slavery became increasingly more repressive over time. By the 1830s and 1840s, nearly every slave state had laws that did not allow enslaved people to read or write. It became more difficult, both legally and economically, for enslaved people to purchase their freedom. Then, in 1857, the U.S. Supreme Court entered slavery's legal arena when it agreed to hear the case of *Dred Scott v. Sanford*. Scott's case, which had worked its way through the legal system (the lower court case was heard in St. Louis) argued that his owner had taken him to Fort Snelling in the future state of Minnesota. At the time, Fort Snelling was part of Wisconsin Territory in which slavery was prohibited by the Missouri Compromise of 1820.

Above:
Auction Broadside,
ca. 1840, from an
unidentified Southern
town announcing a
raffle in which a race
horse and a female
slave are the prizes.

Right:
Dred Scott,
painting after
a photograph,
ca. 1858.

Chief Justice Roger Taney wrote the decision of the court. First he determined that Scott, as an African American, was not a citizen and thus did not have the right to bring a case before the court. The case could have ended there, but Taney went on to find that the Missouri Compromise was unconstitutional because Congress did not have the power to prohibit slavery in the territories. Slaves were property, and the Fifth Amendment protected private property. Taney and the justices in the majority of the Dred Scott Decision no doubt hoped their action would quell the mounting tension over the institution of slavery. The opposite happened.

John Brown, ca. 1856.

'Divorce a Vinculo.' English cartoon, 1861, from Punch on South Carolina's secession from the United States.

The new Republican Party, organized only a few years before, focused its attention on repealing the Dred Scott Decision and prohibiting slavery in all territories. Then in 1859, John Brown, a radical abolitionist, decided to end the institution of slavery on his own. He led a small private army into Harpers Ferry, Virginia, where they intended to take over the federal armory, capture all of the weapons, distribute them to slaves, and lead a rebellion throughout the South. Brown failed. He and most of his rag-tag army were killed or captured. He was executed. But his failure in life became a success in death. At the conclusion of his trial, he prophesied that: "Now, if it is deemed necessary that I should forfeit my life for the furtherance of the ends of justice, and mingle my blood further with the blood of my children and with the blood of millions in this slave country whose rights are disregarded by wicked, cruel, and unjust enactments, I submit; so let it be done!"

A year after John Brown's trial and prophesy, Abraham Lincoln was elected president. A central plank in the Republican Party platform was the prohibition of slavery in the territories. Shortly after Lincoln's election, South Carolina seceded from the Union, followed by 10 other slave states. Then on April 12, 1861, John Brown's prediction came true. The Confederate Army fired on and captured Fort Sumter in Charleston, South Carolina Harbor, starting the Civil War.

Another event—virtually unnoticed at the time—but an event that would soon have profound results took place only six weeks after Fort Sumter. Three enslaved men, Shepard Mallory, Frank Baker, and James Townsend, decided to sneak away from the site where they were forced to work building a Confederate fortification near the mouth of Chesapeake Bay. They commandeered a

Thomas Nast's celebration of the emancipation of Southern slaves with the end of the Civil War. Wood engraving, 1865.

small boat, rowed across the harbor, and surrendered to Union commander Benjamin Butler at Fort Monroe. General Butler determined that since these men were forced to work on a Confederate fort, and since they were enslaved, by definition of the rules of warfare at that time, they were property of the enemy, and thus contraband of war. This story is now told at one of the newest national parks, Fort Monroe National Monument in Virginia. Several national park sites interpret contraband stories including: Fort Donelson National Battlefield in Tennessee, Fort Pickens in Florida, Fort Pulaski National Monument in Georgia, and Anacostia Park and Theodore Roosevelt Island in Washington, D.C.

Historians have debated whether the end to slavery came from the bottom up, with the actions of the three men escaping to Fort Monroe and many others snatching freedom on their own initiative, or from the top down, with the antislavery advocates pressuring the administration to adopt the end of slavery as a war aim. In reality, it was both. By the summer of 1862, President Lincoln decided to add the end of slavery as a final goal of the war, issuing his Emancipation Proclamation, which took effect on January 1, 1863.

Not long after President Lincoln issued the Emancipation Proclamation, the call went out for African American soldiers to serve in the Union army. Before the end of the war, 220,000 black soldiers and sailors served the Union cause. While Union soldiers fought for various reasons—to preserve the Union, for adventure, because they were drafted, to end slavery, and so forth—the goal of African American soldiers was clear. They fought to end slavery, and, in fact, many had escaped from slavery themselves. Furthermore, unlike some Union soldiers who were drafted, all black soldiers and sailors volunteered for service. If white Union soldiers were captured by Confederates, they were held as prisoners of war. If black soldiers were captured, they generally were killed or sold into slavery.

Buffalo Soldiers

In 1866, Congress established six all-black army units—two cavalry regiments and four infantry regiments—each commanded by white officers. These black regiments were sent primarily to western outposts, and before long, they assumed the name "Buffalo Soldiers." The origin of the name is not clear, but it was always used respectfully.

In 1867, Fort Davis, a remote outpost in West Texas abandoned during the Civil War, was one of the first forts garrisoned by the Buffalo Soldiers. They protected the mail and travelers and fought against hostile American Indian tribes. Today, Fort Davis National Historic Site preserves many of the structures in the fort and tells the stories of the Buffalo Soldiers who were stationed there. Fort Larned in Kansas also was remote, built to protect travelers on the Santa Fe Trail. Company A of the 10th Regiment served there from 1867 until 1869. They faced racism from the white soldiers and had duties with other companies that often led to conflicts. Fort Larned National Historic Site interprets the history of the fort and the Buffalo Soldiers.

Buffalo Soldiers also were in other forts and sites that later became national park units. Their service was exemplary in combat soldiery and loyalty. They had lower rates of desertion and alcoholism than other army units at the time. Many completed their five-year enlistments despite the hardships of life on frontier campaigns, the loneliness of garrison duty, and the sting of racism. They were often confronted with racial prejudice from other soldiers and from civilians in the areas where they were stationed, along with the dangers inherent with their soldier duties. Yet, 23 Buffalo Soldiers received Medals of Honor. The Buffalo Soldiers era came to an end on September 6, 2005, when Mark Matthews, the oldest living of the original Buffalo Soldiers, died at the age of 111. He is buried at Arlington National Cemetery.

There were well over 10,000 engagements in the Civil War. The most important of these battle sites are administered by the National Park Service. There is Fort Sumter where the war began; Manassas, the site of the first major land battle; Antietam, at which the largest loss of life in a single day took place and after which Lincoln issued the preliminary Emancipation Proclamation; and Gettysburg, which to most historians was the most decisive of all Civil War battles. One of the lesser-known but important battlefields is Pea Ridge in northwestern Arkansas.

The battle itself was interesting. The Confederates under Gen. Earl Van Dorn were trying to regain control of northern Arkansas and Missouri. In a rare occurrence, Confederates outnumbered the Union troops that were led by Gen. Samuel R. Curtis. In the two-day battle in early March 1862, the Union army won which was a major factor in keeping Missouri in the Union for the remainder of the war.

That's a brief story of the battle. The park interprets two other stories that go beyond who shot whom, where, when, and how. One story is that part of the Confederate army consisted of a number of Cherokee, and also Choctaw, Creek, and Chickasaw Indians who came from Indian

Reenactors depict Buffalo Soldiers at Ft. Davis NHS.

The Trail of Tears, the removal of the Cherokee Native Americans to the West. Oil on canvas, 1942, by Robert Lindneux.

Territory (present-day Oklahoma). Some Creeks, Choctaw, and Cherokees owned African American slaves, something they held in common with many Confederate leaders. But there was another and even more compelling reason why many sided with the South. The Cherokee, Choctaw, Creek, Chickasaw, and Seminole nations had been forcibly removed from their homelands and settled in Indian Territory. Many thought their lands and their futures would be more secure if the Confederacy won the war.

The other story told at Pea Ridge National Military Park further helps to explain why members of these American Indian Nations fought for the Confederacy. Running through the battlefield is the remnant of the "Trail of Tears." This was the route on which some 47,000 Cherokee, Choctaw, Creek, Chickasaw, and Seminole natives were forced to travel after they were forcibly removed from their homelands in the Southeast between 1831 and 1837.

Reconstruction and Repression

An African American sharecropper in Chatham County, North Carolina. Photograph by Dorothea Lange, July 1939.

At the conclusion of the Civil War and with the passage of the Thirteenth, Fourteenth, and Fifteenth Amendments, four million human beings were forever free, they were guaranteed equal protection under the law, and all adult males were guaranteed the right to vote. These freed people made great strides during Reconstruction. They flocked to the newly opened schools throughout the former Confederacy. They held elective offices. They voted. African Americans were beginning to realize the "new birth of freedom" President Lincoln had promised in his Gettysburg Address. Gettysburg National Military Park is where Lincoln's address took place.

Not long after Reconstruction began, former Confederates were able to regain some of their power, and the process of integrating former slaves into American society was put on hold with the election of Rutherford B. Hayes in 1876. Slavery, of course, was illegal, but many plantation owners were creative. They allowed their formerly enslaved people to stay on the land and work as sharecroppers. They could live on the property—often in the quarters they had lived in as slaves—raise crops and then share the profits from the produce. A common practice was for the property owner to run a store from which sharecroppers would buy their goods on credit that theoretically would be paid when the crop was harvested. The sharecropper system lasted well into the 20th century in much of the South and left most sharecroppers in extreme poverty. Cane River Creole National Historical Park and Natchez National Historical Park interpret this story.

Impact of the Homestead Act of 1862

Women's and minorities' rights in the 19th century were extremely limited in most spheres of public and private life, if they existed at all. Incremental social progress was made periodically, but change was accelerated by one piece of legislation: The Homestead Act of 1862. It provided unprecedented opportunity for land ownership to those marginalized by restrictive legislative barriers. It increased the prospects for social and political mobility for women and minorities.

The language of the Homestead Act of 1862 reveals its egalitarian intentions. The authors used "any person," "he or she," "his or her" to describe individuals who would be able to claim 160 acres of free land. The strategic phrasing did not end there. The 37th Congress of the United States, which authored and passed this legislation, intended to encourage immigration to the United States. The very first line of the act says, "That any person...who is a citizen of the United States, or who shall have filed the declaration of intention to become

A poster encouraging westward expansion.

such, as required by the naturalization laws of the United States...shall be entitled to enter one quarter-section (160 acres) or a less quantity of unappropriated public lands...." The extraordinary language needs to be understood in the historical context to know how it truly shifted the paradigm of equality regarding land ownership. The most substantial impact was suffrage, undoubtedly the most cherished right of any citizen in a democracy.

...on Women

States had always retained the right to grant suffrage to its citizenry. States, however, became more proactive in the late 19th and early 20th centuries. Suffrage was first afforded to women in the territory of Wyoming in 1869, followed by the territory of Utah, the state of Idaho, and the state of Colorado by the close of the 19th century. The influx of people seeking free land bolstered the population in these territories and states. Landowners in these regions, many of whom were women, increased exponentially as well. Victories by the women's suffrage movement in the West furthered the national efforts seeking universal suffrage. Homesteading may have provided women more than the opportunity to own land; it may have been one of the catalysts of the women's suffrage movement.

…on Minorities

Prior to the Civil War, African Americans were the most prominent minority in the United States. They could not obtain full citizenship until the ratification of the Fourteenth Amendment in 1868. This was an important feature allowing African Americans to participate in the westward expansion process. The law, as written, was not discriminatory regarding ethnicity. African Americans were free to apply and receive land just like anybody else meeting the requirements of citizenship eligibility. African Americans began to seek opportunities outside the South. Many sought the free land offered by the Homestead Act. This led to a mass exodus by African Americans out of the South. They left the plantations and headed north looking for new opportunities. They were called Exodusters, and most headed to Kansas, in part because they knew this was where John Brown had fought against slavery. The largest concentration of Exodusters settled in western Kansas in a community they called Nicodemus, a symbolic name associated with the biblical personality with whom Jesus talked about being born again. From 1877 into the 1880s,

A building in Nicodemus, Kansas.

the population of Nicodemus grew to over 700. Today, Nicodemus National Historic Site interprets the story of the Exodusters. Promotion and word of mouth had proclaimed that free land was available, and the government was going to ensure passage. But the rumor that free passage was available was false. Thousands of African American potential homesteaders stood stranded on the levees of the Mississippi River near St. Louis, Missouri. Humanitarian efforts led to a national movement seeking to help them. The relief efforts paid off, and many of those who were stranded were finally able to finish their journey. Although the Exoduster Movement lasted only from 1877 to the 1880s, it led to the development of African American homestead communities throughout the West.

…on Immigrants

Immigrant groups from all over the world sought opportunity in the American West. The 37th Congress intended to build an agrarian nation that included individuals from the "Old World." The Homestead Act provided land to any citizen or individual who had "declared their intention to become a citizen." Furthermore, it was written in a manner that provided all the requirements of citizenship; the only caveat was that the immigrant had to be eligible to become a citizen per the naturalization laws. The Homestead Act was not only a land law, but it was also an immigration law. The history of the Homestead Act of 1862 is preserved and told at Homestead National Monument of America.

American Indian Movement

American Indians, starting with Jamestown, were treated badly by the American government. At first, eastern tribes were moved from their homelands farther and farther west. Before the Civil War, nearly all eastern nations were relocated into Indian Territory—except the remnants of larger tribes and several smaller nations. Indian Territory consisted of most of present-day Oklahoma and most of Kansas and Nebraska. As inhumane and horrific as this move was, at least for a time, these tribes were able to remain more or less as cohesive communities. As white settlement filled in more and more western land, starting with removing a number of nations from Kansas and Nebraska, there was less and less land available for relocation. Furthermore, many of the cultures in the West were different. The tribes on the Great Plains were mostly nomadic, following the buffalo herds for their livelihoods. Tribes in arid regions like the Great Basin were nomadic as well and were forced to travel great distances to gather or hunt their food.

For these nomadic tribes, the government's efforts to place them on reservations where they would theoretically become "Christian" farmers was like trying to put round pegs into square holes. They were not, nor had they ever been, farmers. They had no experience living on small parcels of land. And, as if that were not enough, most of the land they were assigned was not very conducive to farming even under the best of circumstances. Not surprisingly, they revolted. Or, in the case of the Cheyenne Indians at Washita (Washita Battlefield National Historic Site) in Oklahoma, the Southern Cheyenne and Southern Arapaho at Sand Creek (Sand Creek Massacre National Historic Site) in Colorado, and the Northern Shoshone at Bear River in Idaho, they were all attacked by U.S. soldiers and massacred with little or no provocation.

The best-known conflict between American Indians and soldiers occurred on the Little Bighorn battlefield in present-day Montana. Col. George Armstrong Custer unwisely led his 7th Cavalry into the valley against several thousand Lakota, Arapaho, and Cheyenne warriors in 1876, and not surprisingly, was annihilated. When the battlefield was set aside as a park and memorial, it was designated as Custer Battlefield National Monument. But, to the American Indians who fought at

15

End of the Battle of Little Bighorn, June 1876. Lower right: Village women prepare a ceremony for the returning warriors. The standing men in the center, left to right: Sitting Bull, Rain-in-the-Face, Crazy Horse, and artist Kicking Bear. Watercolor on muslin, 1898.

Little Bighorn, this battle was a high point in their cultures. So, in 1991, the park was renamed Little Bighorn Battlefield National Monument, and it now recognizes and honors both white soldiers and Indians in the battle that took place there.

The fact that Indian nations pushed for changing the name and the interpretive emphasis of Little Bighorn would have been a surprise to white Americans in the early 1800s. John Quincy Adams, after he had helped negotiate the end of the War of 1812, made the comment that before long the United States would "formally undertake, and accomplish their [the American Indians] utter extermination." By the end of the 19th century, it seemed that perhaps Adams was prophetic. The American Indian population declined from about 600,000 in 1800 to about 250,000 in 1890, due to exotic diseases, warfare, massacres, forced marches to new locations, hunger, and starvation.

The American Indian population has not only survived, but it has increased dramatically since 1890. The 2010 census reported that 2.9 million individuals identified themselves as either American Indian or Native Alaskan, and another 2.3 million called themselves American Indian or Alaska Native in combination with one or more other races. American Indian cultures and many languages have survived as well. In 1924, with the Indian Citizenship Act, Indians gained the right to vote. Through successful court cases in the Pacific Northwest over fishing rights and water rights victories elsewhere, American Indians are exercising their rights to the American legal system. And, finally, Americans are beginning to recognize that perhaps one of the best ways to deal with climate change is to learn to respect their land and surroundings as the American Indians have for centuries.

Women's Movement

Even though women seemed to be beginning to build momentum to achieve their rights at Seneca Falls in 1848, they were thwarted with the passage of the Fifteenth Amendment which enfranchised all adult males but left them out. They would eventually achieve their right to vote with the passage of the Nineteenth Amendment in 1920. The women's movement to achieve the right to vote is celebrated in the Sewall-Belmont House National Historic Site in Washington, D.C.

Although women were denied the basic right to vote and African American women had even more difficult prejudices to conquer, two women, celebrated in two national park units, beat the odds. Maggie L. Walker was born shortly after the end of the Civil War in Richmond, Virginia. Her mother was a slave and a cook in one of Richmond's grand mansions. Maggie taught school and then left the classroom to raise her family. She became an active leader in the Independent Order of

Cover of Leslie's Illustrated Newspaper, *September 11, 1920, shortly after the ratification of the 19th Amendment.*

St. Luke, a philanthropic organization, and later became the first African American female bank president and one of the first women to charter a bank in the United States. (Maggie L. Walker National Historic Site)

Maggie Lena Walker

Mary McLeod Bethune was born shortly after the Civil War to parents who had been enslaved. She attended college and then started a school for African American girls in Daytona Beach, Florida. From six students it grew and merged with an institute for African American boys and eventually became the Bethune-Cookman University. She served as president of the college for over 20 years and was one of the few women in the world who served as a college president at that time. She founded the National Council of Negro Women and advised President Franklin Roosevelt on racial issues. (Mary McLeod Bethune Council House National Historic Site and Mary McLeod Bethune Memorial, both in Washington, D.C.)

As educators, Mary McLeod Bethune and Maggie L. Walker taught in segregated schools. Although the Fourteenth Amendment seemingly provided for and meant that all Americans would have equal protection under the law, in 1896, in the landmark Supreme Court decision—*Plessy v. Ferguson*—the court decided that for all public facilities, schools, public transportation, restrooms, etc., they could be separate but also equal for blacks and whites. But what exactly was equal if both races were treated separately?

NAACP and the National Urban League Take Action

During the early years of the National Park Service in the 1920s and 1930s, national park facilities were segregated in keeping with local customs and Jim Crow laws, particularly in the Southern states. Some sites even discouraged African Americans from using the parks. This attitude and practice also extended to some of the larger western parks. Some parks were reluctant even to provide segregated facilities such as campgrounds. The leadership of the NAACP and the National Urban League opposed these attitudes and practices and petitioned the leadership of the Department of the Interior and the National Park Service to provide facilities for African Americans.

In a June 1933 letter to Secretary of the Interior Harold Ickes, Acting Executive Secretary of the National Urban League T. Arnold Hill stated, "Few needs of the great mass of southern Negroes are so completely underserved as those of recreation." Since many local, regional, and other parks during this period were not open to African Americans, Hill proposed to Ickes, that "park projects be planned for states in the deep south that will definitely take care of the Negroes which will offer camping, hiking and picnic sites."

The NAACP and the National Urban League would continue to push for fully accessible park facilities and would have in W.J. Trent, Jr., a strong advocate. Trent served as adviser on negro affairs to Secretary Ickes and was also a member of the NAACP and the National Urban League.

In 1945, Ickes issued a Secretarial Order banning any form of segregation and discrimination in the public's use of national park facilities, including those operated by concessioners. Secretary Ickes took this action well before the Civil Rights Act of 1964.

Left to right: NAACP attorneys George E.C. Hayes, Thurgood Marshall, and James Nabrit, Jr., celebrate their victory in the Brown vs. the Board of Education *case at the Supreme Court in Washington, D.C.*

"Separate but Equal"

In the 1940s and 1950s, activists—in particular the NAACP—began to knock chinks in the armor around *Plessy*. The strategy was to demonstrate that equal meant equal, not sort of, kind of, or pretty much equal. In the case of *Sweatt v. Painter* (1950), Heman Marion Sweatt, who was qualified for but denied admission to the University of Texas Law School, argued that although the State of Texas had made a good faith effort to establish a law school for African Americans, the education he would receive there would not be "equal" to the University of Texas. For example, the University of Texas had over 65,000 volumes in its law library, whereas the Texas State University for Negroes Law School had only 16,500 volumes. The University of Texas Law School had graduates in public and private practice all over the state, but only one African American was admitted to the Texas bar at the time. Thus, the Supreme Court found that here "separate" did not meet the standard of equal.

Thurgood Marshall had been denied admission to the University of Maryland Law School, and instead attended Howard University Law School in Washington, D.C. As an attorney for the NAACP, overturning *Plessy* became a crusade for him. In the early 1950s, the strategy shifted slightly to a position that no matter how "equal" any facilities were—particularly segregated public schools—they were still unequal. The NAACP combined several school segregation cases together under *Brown v. Board of Education* and appealed to the U.S. Supreme Court to overturn *Plessy*. The *Brown* case had particular appeal since it came from a segregated school district in the North. In a unanimous decision, written by Chief Justice Earl Warren, the Supreme Court found in 1954 that "separate educational facilities are inherently unequal." The court further found that the plaintiffs were "deprived of the equal protection of the laws guaranteed by the Fourteenth Amendment."

One hundred fifty years before *Brown*, the First Amendment was written and the courts interpreted that individual civil liberties were protected only from federal actions. Shortly after World War I, however, this paradigm began to change. The Supreme Court began to incorporate the rights and freedoms guaranteed in the Constitution to state and local actions under the equal protection clause of the Fourteenth Amendment. Thus, the *Brown* decision was, in part tied to the equal protection clause. Furthermore, unlike the language of the First Amendment, "Congress shall make no law respecting…," the Thirteenth, Fourteenth and most subsequent amendments, provided that "Congress shall have power to enforce, by appropriate legislation, the provisions of this article."

World War II Internment of Japanese Americans

Wartime in the United States almost always tamped down civil liberties and civil rights. President Lincoln suspended the writ of *habeas corpus* in certain areas of the country during the Civil War. Freedom of speech and the press were often curtailed. But perhaps the most heinous of all abuses to civil rights in the 20th century was launched against Japanese Americans during World War II. After the Japanese attack on Pearl Harbor, there was widespread fear all along the West Coast that the Japanese military would follow up its attack on the American mainland. Furthermore, and with absolutely no evidence, white Americans on the West Coast feared that Japanese Americans were spies for the Japanese government. The American military, with the full support of California Attorney General Earl Warren—the same Earl Warren, who as chief justice wrote the decision in *Brown v. Board of Education*—recommended to President Franklin D. Roosevelt that all Japanese Americans on the Pacific Coast be placed in concentration camps for the duration of the war.

With Executive Order 9066, issued on February 19, 1942, President Roosevelt authorized internment. Local military commanders could designate "military areas" as "exclusion zones" from which "any or all persons may be excluded." What this meant was that all people of Japanese ancestry were "excluded" from all of California and much of Oregon, Washington, and Arizona. Hawaii was exempted from the ruling, although the 150,000 residents of Japanese ancestry made up about one-third of the entire population. Over 60 percent of Japanese Americans placed in these camps were American citizens.

More than 110,000 Japanese Americans were forced to leave their homes, jobs, and businesses with very little time to settle their affairs, report to assembly centers, and then be transferred to "relocation centers" in some of the most godforsaken areas of the United States. These relocation centers were little more than prisons or concentration camps, and these places were their homes for the duration of the war. Several Japanese Americans challenged the executive order in court, seeking writs of *habeas corpus*, but the Supreme Court upheld the order. Of the 10 primary relocation centers, three—Manzanar (Manzanar National Historic Site) and Tule Lake (a unit of World War II Valor in the Pacific National Monument) in California, and Minidoka (Minidoka National Historic Site) in Idaho—interpret this horrific time in our history as units of the National Park Service.

Members of the American Legion and Boy Scouts at a Memorial Day ceremony at the Manzanar Relocation Center for Japanese Americans, 1942.

Discrimination in the Military

Earlier, we discussed the African American soldiers and sailors who fought for the Union in the Civil War and the Buffalo Soldiers who served in the West and who administered national parks after the war. Between that time and World War II, the nation went backwards in its racial issues. By World War II, African American soldiers and sailors were pretty much relegated to support positions. There were exceptions. One of the most important was the creation of the African American Tuskegee Airmen who trained at the Tuskegee Institute in Alabama and flew primarily as bomber escorts in Europe. Their record was remarkable, and as their record for escorting bombers grew, whenever bomber crews saw the distinctive red tails of the P-47 and later P-51 Mustang fighters, they knew they were being protected by the "Red-Tail Angels." Their stories are told at Tuskegee Airmen National Historic Site.

Not all African American military stories had the positive outcome of the Tuskegee Airmen. On the evening of July 17, 1944, the Port Chicago naval munitions base located on San Francisco Bay, became the site of the largest stateside military disaster of WWII when a horrific explosion that measured 3.4 on the Richter scale killed 320 men and injured another 390 men.

Of the 320 men who were killed, 202 were African Americans. After the tragedy, many of the survivors were transferred to other facilities, including over 300 men, mostly African American, who were ordered onto the loading pier of the Mare Island naval facility a few miles away. Most of the black sailors refused the order, citing continued lack of training and the same poor equipment as was used at Port Chicago—thus the clear possibility of another explosion. Some 250 African American sailors who refused the transfer orders were arrested and charged with mutiny. About 200 reluctantly agreed to return to duty, but the 50 others who still refused to load munitions remained in custody with mutiny charges hanging over their heads. In the courts-martial that followed, all 50 sailors were found guilty and sentenced to prison terms from eight to fifteen years. All received dishonorable discharges.

After the trial, Thurgood Marshall sought and failed to have the convictions overturned. When the war ended a year later, and the spirit of peace prevailed, President Harry S Truman finally agreed to release the men under a general amnesty and time served. Upon their release, though, the men were never granted navy veterans' benefits, and their felony convictions were upheld, as were their dishonorable discharges from the navy.

The dual tragedies of the Port Chicago explosion and courts-martial of the African American sailors vividly illustrated racial discrimination in the military establishment and fueled public criticism. It became a major step in the decision by President Truman to desegregate the armed forces in 1948.

Tuskegee Airmen at a briefing at Ramitelli Airfield, Italy, March 1945.

Birth of the Civil Rights Movement

The progress toward civil rights was growing after World War II. President Truman integrated the armed forces. The Supreme Court unanimously decided that separate but equal had absolutely nothing to do with equality. On December 1, 1955, shortly after the court decided *Brown v. Board of Education*, an African American woman in Montgomery, Alabama, decided that she did not want to give up her seat on a city bus to a white person. "People always say that I didn't give up my seat because I was tired, but that isn't true," Rosa Parks said later. She continued, "the only tired I was, was tired of giving in." For refusing to give up her seat, Mrs. Parks was arrested. Several days later, the black leaders in Montgomery organized a bus boycott and elected a young, recent arrival in town by the name of Dr. Martin Luther King, Jr., who was the minister of the Dexter Avenue Baptist Church, as the head of the Montgomery Improvement Association.

Rosa Parks fingerprinted by Lieutenant Drue H. Lackey in Montgomery, Alabama, February 22, 1956, following her arrest.

The bus strike lasted over a year, causing great hardship to many African Americans who relied on the bus as their only means of transportation. It also put a strain on the bus company, with many of its buses sitting idle, and a large segment of its ridership boycotting. Finally Montgomery repealed its law, thus integrating its bus system. To many, this really was the beginning of the civil rights movement. Rosa Parks became one of the most iconic figures in 20th-century America, and Dr. Martin Luther King, Jr. became the leader of the national civil rights movement.

In September 1957, Arkansas Governor Orval Faubus defied the order to integrate all-white Central High School in Little Rock. President Eisenhower sent in federal troops to intervene and ensure that the African American "Little Rock Nine" could attend school. (Little Rock Central High School National Historic Site) In February 1960, four black students from Agricultural & Technical College of North Carolina sat at Woolworth's lunch counter in Greensboro, North Carolina. They were not served, but they did not leave either—beginning a sit-in movement in the South.

In May 1961, about 1,000 students tested the new ban on segregation of interstate travel by riding buses throughout the South. James Meredith, an African American student, entered the University of Mississippi in 1962, and President Kennedy sent in 5,000 troops to protect him. The year 1963 was momentous. Medgar Evers, an officer in the Mississippi NAACP, was murdered in Jackson, Mississippi. Some 200,000 people gathered at the Lincoln Memorial in August to hear the Rev. Martin Luther King, Jr. deliver his immortal "I Have a Dream" speech. Earlier that year, the nation witnessed the bare-knuckled brutality against African Americans in Birmingham, Alabama, directed by Commissioner of Public Safety Eugene "Bull" Connor. And four young black girls were murdered when a bomb went off in Sixteenth Street Baptist Church, also in Birmingham.

All of this led to the passage of the Civil Rights Act of 1964, the most sweeping civil rights legislation since Reconstruction, prohibiting discrimination of all kinds based on race, color, religion, or national origin. The law also provided the federal government with the powers to enforce desegregation. A year later, in March 1965, African Americans and others organized a march

Martin Luther King, Jr. at the March on Washington, August 28, 1963.

in Alabama from Selma to Birmingham. They were stopped at the Edmund Pettus Bridge by police who brutally beat the marchers, sending 50 to the hospital. "Black Sunday" was widely covered by the media and was an impetus for the Voting Rights Act of 1965 that did away with literacy tests, poll taxes, and other requirements that were used to restrict black voting.

César Chávez and the United Farm Workers Movement

César Chávez, ca. 1970.

Although the Civil Rights Act of 1964 prohibited discrimination of any kind, it would take some time before Latino farm workers in the agricultural areas of California, Texas, and elsewhere, who were forced to move from one area to another to pick crops—cotton in the fall, peas and lettuce in the winter, and so forth—to begin to enjoy the blessings of this act. They received meager wages, lived in shabby migrant worker housing, and their children generally received very little education. Such had been the life of César Chávez growing up in Arizona and California. His family was forced from their home in Arizona during the depression and moved to California where they were migrant workers. Chávez left school after the eighth grade to help his family make ends meet.

Chávez worked in the fields until 1952 when he joined the Community Service Organization as a champion of Latino workers' rights and to also encourage farm workers to vote. From that experience, in 1962, he organized the National Farm Workers Association with Dolores Huerta, which eventually became the United Farm Workers. He organized strikes in the grape-growing areas of California and encouraged boycotts by Americans from buying table grapes. The United Farm Workers successfully lobbied for the passage of the California Agricultural Labor Relations Act which gave collective bargaining rights to farm workers. During the 1980s, Chávez led a boycott to protest the use of toxic pesticides on grapes. As a leader of his movement, Chávez borrowed non-violent protest styles from Gandhi and Martin Luther King, Jr. He often would fast for days in support of a cause. To celebrate his life and to commemorate his amazing accomplishments, César E. Chávez National Monument was designated as the 398th unit of the National Park System in 2012.

Gains in Civil Rights and Liberties for All

In the 1960s, gay rights groups throughout the country became more militant. They began speaking out against police entrapment and working to educate the public about homosexuality. They fought against discrimination in government employment to counter earlier McCarthyism linking of Communist subversion and homosexuality. The Stonewall riot during a June 1969 police raid on the Stonewall Inn in Greenwich Village in New York City, traditionally marks the beginning of the Gay Liberation Movement, although the emergence was in fact more gradual and more complex. In the aftermath of the riot, gay liberation fronts spread from New York to other major cities and college campuses across the country. Women broke away from male-dominated organizations to form lesbian feminist groups and collectives. The struggle shifted from the right to public space to education, including the demand for gay and lesbian studies in universities; legal protection for gay, lesbian, bisexual and eventually, transgender (LGBT) people; and equal employment, including in schools, the military, and government. The modern LGBT movement emerged from this period of activism. In 1974, the first federal civil rights bill for gay men and lesbians was introduced in Congress.

In 1990, the Americans with Disabilities Act extended the "powers, remedies, and procedures" of the Civil Rights Act of 1964 to disabled Americans to prohibit discrimination in employment, public accommodations, and other matters.

In 2008, Barack Obama was elected 44th president of the United States, 148 years after another Illinoisan, Abraham Lincoln, was elected 16th president. In 1860, it would have been inconceivable, and in most states illegal, for Mr. Obama, as an African American man, to vote or hold office. One hundred forty-eight years seems a long time. In 2011, Frank Buckles, the oldest surviving U.S. veteran of World War I, died at age 110. When Buckles was four, Hiram Cronk, the oldest surviving U.S. veteran of the War of 1812 died at age 105. So the lives of these two men spanned 210 years, from the John Adams administration to the Obama administration. Maybe 148 years really isn't that long. Furthermore, in 2013, 18 women serve in the U.S. Senate. In 1964, when the Civil Rights Act was passed, only one woman served in the Senate.

Barack Obama, 44th president of the United States.

—Text by NPS Chief Historian Robert K. Sutton. Text on the Homestead Act by Historian Blake Bell, Homestead NM of America.

A band of slaves marched into town for sale. Illustration from an American abolitionist publication, 1835.

The Journey Continues

Though progress has been made in the arena of civil rights for
Americans, the journey is ongoing. Your national parks manage
and interpret many of the important sites along the way. We invite
you to visit, learn, and understand the progress that has been
made. Although the journey is long, the future looks promising.

On the following pages park sites that emphasize the civil rights
story are highlighted. There are many other
sites that interpret various aspects of the
struggle for civil rights in the United States.
For more information on these and other
national park sites visit www.nps.gov

A civil rights protest march in New York, 1965.

Suffragists picketing the White House, 1917.

African American Civil War Memorial

1925 Vermont Avenue NW
Washington, DC 20001
202- 667-2667
www.nps.gov/afam

At the beginning of the American Civil War, there were many who felt the conflict should solely be a struggle to preserve the Union and be exclusively a white man's fight. As the war progressed, though, and runaway slaves continued to flee to Federal armies in greater numbers, more people began to feel that something should be done about this "curious institution" known as slavery. Early on, Congress forbad the enlistment of free African Americans and only allowed the use of former slaves as workers in the military.

With the passage of the Second Confiscation Act and the Militia Act in July 1862, African Americans from anywhere in the country were sanctioned to join the U.S. military and contribute to the cause that some now saw as a struggle for a "new birth of freedom." Over 200,000 African American soldiers and sailors served to keep the United States whole and to free permanently over four million people in forced servitude. Through their valor, service, and sacrifice during the war, black soldiers and sailors disproved the claims of African American inferiority and laid the groundwork for the future struggles in citizenship and voting rights that would continue for over one hundred years.

The African American Civil War Memorial honors the service and sacrifices of those individuals who played their part in helping their people and their country.

The "Spirit of Freedom" statue is dedicated to African Americans who served in the Civil War.

Alcatraz Island

Golden Gate National Recreation Area
Fort Mason, Building 201
San Francisco, California 94123
415-561-4700
www.nps.gov/alca

Based on oral history, it appears that Alcatraz Island (originally called *Alcatraces*, named after the Brown Pelican seen in the area by Spanish explorers) was used as a place of isolation for tribal members who had violated a tribal law or taboo, an area for gathering foods, and a hiding place for American Indians attempting to escape from the California Mission system.

On November 19, 1969, American Indians once again came to Alcatraz Island

Alcatraz Indian occupation.

when Richard Oakes, a Mohawk, and a group of American Indian supporters set out in a chartered boat to symbolically claim the island. On November 20, 1969, this symbolic occupation turned into a full-scale occupation which lasted until June, 1971. On June 10, armed federal marshals, FBI agents, and Special Forces police swarmed the island and ended the occupation. This 19-month operation is the longest prolonged occupation of a federal facility by American Indians.

The success or failure of the occupation should not be judged by whether the demands of the occupiers were realized. The under-

lying goals of the American Indians were to awaken the American public to the plight of the first Americans and to assert the need for American Indian self-determination. The result was that the official government policy of termination of tribes was ended, and a policy of American Indian self-determination became the official U.S. government policy. Alcatraz may have been lost, but the occupation gave birth to a political movement which continues today.

Andrew Johnson
National Historic Site

101 North College Street
Greeneville, Tennessee 37743
423-638-3551
www.nps.gov/anjo

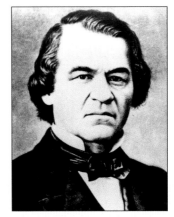

Andrew Johnson, 17th president of the United States.

Andrew Johnson, a Southerner from Tennessee, was a man of many seeming contradictions. He firmly believed in the Union, yet he believed that many political decisions should be left to the individual states. As a slave owner, he was a product of his time.

On January 1, 1863, Abraham Lincoln's Emancipation Proclamation freed slaves in states still in rebellion against the United States. Tennessee, although a seceded state, did not fall under the provisions of the proclamation. Tennessee was under Union control; Johnson was serving as military governor. He freed his personal slaves on August 8, 1863. On October 24, 1864, he freed all the slaves in the state of Tennessee. August 8 has continued to be recognized as a holiday in the African American community in Tennessee and surrounding states.

As vice president of the United States in 1865, Johnson succeeded Abraham Lincoln following Lincoln's assassination. As the 17th president of the United States (1865-1869), he presided over the initial and contentious Reconstruction era following the American Civil War. His Reconstruction policies failed to promote the rights of the newly freed slaves, and he came under political attack from Republicans, ending in his impeachment by the U.S. House of Representatives. He was acquitted by the U.S. Senate.

Andrew Johnson National Historic Site interprets the life and legacy of Andrew Johnson. It illustrates the U.S. Constitution at work and the attempts to reunify a nation torn apart by civil war. Johnson's presidency helped shaped the future of the United States, and his influences continue today.

An old postcard of the Andrew Johnson NHS Visitor Center.

Boston National Historical Park

Faneuil Hall Visitor Center
(near Government Center Plaza at Congress and North Streets)
Boston, Massachusetts 02109
617-242-5642
www.nps.gov/bost

African Meeting House, ca. 1890.

Goods and ideas have flowed for centuries through the port of Boston. It is the same port that has been defended so fiercely and has inspired so many to stand up for their civil rights and liberties.

Begin your visit at historic Faneuil Hall which has served as a marketplace and a meeting hall since 1742. There you will be guided to Boston African American National Historic Site, the Freedom Trail, and other historic sites which commemorate the quest for freedom, civil rights, and liberties in Boston from colonial to modern times.

Boston African American National Historic Site preserves and interprets the history of the free black community in antebellum Boston. This community, living on Beacon Hill along with its white allies, led the nation in the struggle to abolish slavery. Take a tour of the Black Heritage Trail. Sites along the trail include the homes, schools, churches, and gathering places of this remarkable community. The African Meeting House, which opened in 1806, served as the spiritual, cultural, and political center of this community. The Lewis and Harriet Hayden House played an integral role in Boston's Underground Railroad. The Abiel Smith School is the first schoolhouse in the nation built for the sole purpose of educating black students. Augustus Saint-Gaudens's masterpiece, the Robert Gould Shaw Memorial, is where the trail begins and honors Shaw and the bravery and sacrifice of the 54th Massachusetts Infantry, the first Northern black regiment to serve in the Civil War.

Bunker Hill Monument

Bunker Hill Museum exhibits

Brown v. Board of Education National Historic Site

1515 SE Monroe Street
Topeka, Kansas 66612
785-354-4273
www.nps.gov/brvb

Monroe Elementary School after restoration.

On May 17, 1954, the U.S. Supreme Court decision in *Brown v. Board of Education of Topeka* unanimously ruled that racial segregation in schools was unconstitutional. The ruling overturned the 1896 *Plessy v. Ferguson* decision that had approved the "separate but equal doctrine." The case from Topeka was one of five cases challenging racial segregation in public education. The other cases were from Delaware, the District of Columbia, South Carolina, and Virginia. The court combined the cases into one class action suit. Supreme Court Justice Tom Clark remembers listing the Kansas case first to show that the issue was not "purely a Southern one."

Thurgood Marshall, chief counsel of the NAACP Legal Defense and Education Fund and later the first African American Supreme Court justice, played a critical role in the presentation and argument of the cases. African American psychologists Kenneth B. Clark and his wife, Mamie Phipps Clark, prepared research that helped the Supreme Court rule that "separate educational facilities are inherently unequal."

The park is located in the former Monroe Elementary School where Linda Brown attended school. Her father, Oliver Brown, was the first of 13 plaintiffs listed in the Kansas case. The school has been restored to its 1954 appearance and contains interactive exhibits, films, and a bookstore. Park rangers greet visitors and give them an introduction to the story of *Brown v. Board of Education*.

Reenactors at Brown v. Board of Education National Historic Site.

Cane River Creole National Historical Park

Oakland Plantation, 4386 Highway 494
Bermuda, Louisiana 71456
318-356-8441
www.nps.gov/cari

Magnolia Plantation slave/tenant quarters.

Secession, Civil War, and Reconstruction brought about many changes in the Cane River area, politically, economically, and socially. Crops, lands, and lives were lost. Enslaved workers found new opportunities as freed people to stay, move on, or reestablish themselves on new plantations. Planter families were forced to negotiate labor contracts with freedmen that gave way to agricultural systems of sharecropping and tenant farming. As Magnolia Plantation's ginning equipment and general farm equipment were modernized, sharecropping and tenant systems were phased out. This signaled the beginning of the end of the area's plantation system.

Cane River Creole National Historical Park interprets plantation life. The site includes several quarters in which enslaved people lived and two plantations: Oakland and Magnolia. Both demonstrate the history of colonization, frontier influences, French Creole architecture and culture, cotton agriculture, slavery, and social practices over 200 years. The Cane River region is home to a unique culture: the Creoles. The relationship between the Cane River Creoles and their homeland was shaped by the river. This relationship was tested by flood, drought, war, and numerous other obstacles. Fortunately, their resilience and resourcefulness has allowed the Creole culture to endure and thrive. The park is part of the 40,000-acre Cane River National Heritage Area.

Slave quarters fireplace before restoration.

Oakland Plantation store.

César E. Chávez
National Monument

29700 Woodford-Tehachapi Road
Keene, California 93531
661-823-6134
www.nps.gov/cech

USPS stamp honoring
César E. Chávez.

César E. Chávez, widely recognized as the most important Latino leader in the United States during the 20th century, led farm workers and supporters in the establishment of the country's first permanent agricultural union. His leadership brought sustained international attention to the plight of U.S. farm workers and secured for them higher wages and safer working conditions.

Under the leadership of Chávez and others, such as Dolores Huerta and Larry Itliong, along with support from millions of Americans, the farm worker movement joined forces with other reform movements to achieve unprecedented successes that greatly improved working and living conditions and wages for farm workers. During the 1970s, the United Farm Workers of America grew and expanded from its early roots as a union for farm workers to become a national voice for the poor and disenfranchised. The enduring legacies of César Chávez and the farm worker movement include passage of California's Agricultural Labor Relations Act of 1975, the first law in the United States that recognized farm workers' collective bargaining rights.

Chávez flanked by photos of Robert Kennedy and Mahatma Gandhi.

31

The monument is the fourth national monument designated by President Obama using the Antiquities Act. The National Park Service manages the national monument as the 398th unit of the National Park System in cooperation with the National Chávez Center. The site includes a visitor center and a memorial garden in which Chávez is buried. The National Chávez Center at La Paz continues to be a home and workplace just as it was during Chávez's life. Visitors are asked to respect the privacy of the farm worker movement organizations that still operate from this site and the residents who live here.

Robert Kennedy visits César Chávez during one of Chávez's hunger strikes.

Eleanor Roosevelt National Historic Site

4097 Albany Post Road
Hyde Park, New York 12538
845-229-9115
www.nps.gov/elro

First Lady Eleanor Roosevelt

Eleanor Roosevelt National Historic Site commemorates the life of an outstanding woman in American history and her work on the issues and humanitarian concerns to which she devoted her considerable intellect. She was First Lady of the United States, a United Nations delegate, and chair of the United Nations Commission on Human Rights. As a private citizen, she spoke out against racism; injustice; political, economic, and social inequality; and oppression.

Her legacy is showcased through her writings, her address on human rights to the United Nations, and the introductory film, *Eleanor Roosevelt: Close to Home*, that is shown in the playhouse. Tour Val-Kill, Mrs. Roosevelt's home, and stroll the grounds. Val-Kill was originally a furniture factory started by Mrs. Roosevelt to teach young men from the area a trade during the Depression. When the factory closed in 1936, Mrs. Roosevelt converted it into

Statue of Eleanor Roosevelt at FDR Memorial, Washington, D.C.

a retreat home. It became her permanent residence after the death in 1945 of her husband, Franklin Delano Roosevelt, the 32nd president of the United States. It was here that she pursued her political and social interests, wrote her "My Day" column, and worked on the Universal Declaration of Human Rights. The declaration was ratified in 1948 and details all rights that every human being should possess. She called this her proudest achievement.

32

Federal Hall
National Memorial

26 Wall Street
New York, New York 10005
212-825-6990
www.nps.gov/feha

This building is on the site of New York City's 18th-century City Hall where the 1735 trial of John Peter Zenger was held. He was jailed, tried, and acquitted of libel for exposing government corruption in his newspaper. It was an early victory for freedom of the press. City Hall hosted the Stamp Act Congress, which assembled in October 1765 to protest "taxation without representation." After the American Revolution, the Continental Congress met at City Hall and in 1787, adopted the Northwest Ordinance, establishing procedures for creating new states.

When the Constitution was ratified in 1788, New York remained the national capital. Pierre L'Enfant was commissioned to remodel City Hall for the new federal government. The First Congress met in the (now) Federal Hall and wrote the Bill of Rights. George Washington was inaugurated here as the country's first president on April 30, 1789. When the capital moved to Philadelphia in 1790, the building again housed city government until 1812, when Federal Hall was demolished. The present building was completed in 1842.

Today the building serves as a museum and memorial to George Washington and the beginnings of the United States of America.

33

Federal Hall today.

Fort Raleigh
National Historic Site

c/o Cape Hatteras National Seashore
1401 National Park Drive
Manteo, North Carolina 27954
252-473-5772
www.nps.gov/fora

Queen Elizabeth I

The first English attempts at colonization in the New World are commemorated at Fort Raleigh National Historic Site. Led by Governor John White and sponsored by Sir Walter Raleigh, the colonists departed from England on May 8, 1587. Instead of traveling to their intended destination on the Chesapeake Bay, however, they disembarked at Roanoke Island. Plagued with a shortage of food and supplies and unable to coexist peaceably with the American Indians, the colony experienced difficulty from the outset. On August 27, 1587, just 37 days after the colonists arrived on the Carolina coast, Governor White left the settlement and returned to England for supplies. The outbreak of war with Spain thwarted his plans for prompt relief for the colony. He did not return to Roanoke Island until 1590, at which time he found the settlement abandoned. Because of inclement weather and his own lack of authority, his fellow voyagers aborted their search for the colonists and returned to England. The disappearance of this colony sometime between John White's departure in August 1587 and his return in 1590 is one of the enduring mysteries of American history.

The site also celebrates the preservation of American Indian culture and was the location of an important freedmen's colony during the Civil War era. The American tradition of persistence and courage in the face of great adversity was defined by actions on these grounds and continues to thrive in our national spirit.

Sir Walter Raleigh

Wayside exhibit at Fort Raleigh earthworks.

Fort Sumter
National Monument

1214 Middle Street
Sullivan's Island, South Carolina 29482
843-883-3123
www.nps.gov/fosu

When the Civil War finally exploded in Charleston Harbor on April 12, 1861, it was the result of a half-century of growing sectionalism. Escalating crises over property rights, human rights, states' rights, and constitutional rights divided the country as it expanded westward. Underlying all the economic, social, and political rhetoric was the volatile question of slavery. Because South Carolina's

Fort Sumter before the first shot.

economic life had long depended on enslaved labor, it was the first state to secede. Confederate forces fired the first shot in South Carolina, and the Federal government responded with force. Decades of compromise were over, and the very nature of the Union was at stake.

Fort Sumter exhibits tell the story of the fort and island, events leading to the April 1861 battle, and the subsequent bombardment and reduction of Fort Sumter by artillery later in the war. Read the text of the exhibit at the Fort Sumter Visitor Education Center at Liberty Square in Charleston about events leading up to the first shots fired at Fort Sumter. Use the self-guiding brochure and interpretive wayside exhibits to tour Fort Moultrie's history from the American Revolution through World War II.

There is an entrance fee for Fort Moultrie, but none for Fort Sumter. Fort Sumter is located on an island in Charleston Harbor and is accessible only by boat. Sullivan's Island is the park's mailing address and the location of park headquarters and Fort Moultrie. Visitors without their own boats cannot get to Fort Sumter from Sullivan's Island or Fort Moultrie. A concession-operated ferry service takes visitors to Fort Sumter from Liberty Square in Charleston and Patriots Point in Mount Pleasant.

Artillery at the fort.

Frederick Douglass National Historic Site

1411 W Street, SE
Washington, DC 20020
202-426-5961
www.nps.gov/frdo

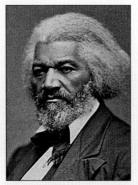

Frederick Douglass

Born into slavery in 1818, Frederick Douglass was taught to read by his owner's wife, thus encouraging him to pursue an education. He eventually escaped to spend his adult life fighting for justice and equality for all people, whether black, female, American Indian, or immigrant.

In 1847, Douglass began publication of *The North Star* weekly newspaper in Rochester, New York, and became an eloquent and passionate spokesman for emancipation and women's rights. He helped runaway slaves find freedom using the Underground Railroad. He worked to aid the Union cause and met with President Lincoln to improve the treatment of African American soldiers. Frederick Douglass's accomplishments were many. As one of our nation's outstanding thinkers, writers, and orators, he became one of the 19th century's most tireless civil rights advocates and social reformers. He famously was quoted as saying, "I would unite with anybody to do right and with nobody to do wrong." His brilliant words and inclusive vision of humanity continue to inspire and sustain people today.

Frederick Douglass National Historic Site preserves the Cedar Hill Estate home and legacy of Frederick Douglass: runaway slave, abolitionist, author, publisher, statesman, college trustee, and champion of human rights.

Cedar Hill Estate today.

Gettysburg National Military Park

1195 Baltimore Pike, Suite 100
Gettysburg, Pennsylvania 17325
717-334-1124
www.nps.gov/gett

Illustration of Lincoln delivering The Gettysburg Address.

The Battle of Gettysburg, fought July 1-3, 1863, brought devastation to Gettysburg. Every farm field or garden was a graveyard. Churches, public buildings, and private homes were hospitals for the wounded. Prominent Gettysburg residents, concerned with the poor condition of soldiers' graves scattered over the battlefield and at hospital sites, pleaded for state support to purchase a portion of the battlefield to be set aside as a final resting place for the defenders of the Union cause. Removal of the dead to the new Soldiers' National Cemetery began in fall 1863 but was not completed until long after the cemetery grounds were dedicated on November 19, 1863. President Abraham Lincoln provided the ceremony's most notable words in his two-minute-long address eulogizing the Union soldiers buried at Gettysburg and reminding those attending the dedication of the soldiers' sacrifice for the Union cause. In his address, he invoked the principles of human equality contained in the Declaration of Independence and connected the sacrifices of the Civil War with a new birth of freedom, preservation of the Union, and its ideal of self-government.

In 1864, the Gettysburg Battlefield Memorial Association was established to preserve portions of the battlefield as a memorial. In 1895, the association transferred its land holdings to the federal government, which designated Gettysburg as a national military park. A federally appointed commission of Civil War veterans oversaw the park's development as a memorial to both the Union and Confederate armies. In 1933, park administration was transferred from the War Department to the National Park Service which continues its mission to protect, preserve, and interpret the Battle of Gettysburg and the Gettysburg Address to park visitors.

THE GETTYSBURG ADDRESS

DELIVERED BY ABRAHAM LINCOLN NOV. 19 1863

AT THE DEDICATION SERVICES ON THE BATTLE FIELD

Fourscore and seven years ago our fathers brought forth on this continent a new nation, conceived in liberty, and dedicated to the proposition that all men are created equal. ✶ ✶ ✶ Now we are engaged in a great civil war, testing whether that nation, or any nation so conceived and so dedicated, can long endure. ✶ ✶ We are met on a great battle-field of that war. ✶ We have come to dedicate a portion of that field as a final resting place for those who here gave their lives that that nation might live. ✶ ✶ It is altogether fitting and proper that we should do this. ✶ ✶ But in a larger sense we cannot dedicate, we cannot consecrate, we cannot hallow this ground. ✶ The brave men, living and dead, who struggled here, have consecrated it far above our poor power to add or detract. The world will little note, nor long remember, what we say here, but it can never forget what they did here. ✶ ✶ It is for us, the living, rather to be dedicated here to the unfinished work which they who fought here have thus far so nobly advanced It is rather for us to be here dedicated to the great task remaining before us, that from these honored dead we take increased devotion to that cause for which they gave the last full measure of devotion; ✶ that we here highly resolve that these dead shall not have died in vain; that this nation, under God, shall have a new birth of freedom, and that the government of the people, by the people, and for the people, shall not perish from the earth

Harpers Ferry National Historical Park

171 Shoreline Drive
Harpers Ferry, West Virginia 25425
304-535-6029
www.nps.gov/hafe

Reenactor discharges weapon.

Harpers Ferry witnessed John Brown's attack on slavery, the largest surrender of Federal troops during the Civil War, and the education of former slaves in one of the earliest integrated schools in the United States.

In October 1867, the Reverend Dr. Nathan Cook Brackett established a Freewill Baptist primary school, "Storer Normal School," in the Lockwood House, a former armory residence, on Camp Hill. Brackett's tireless efforts to establish freedmen's schools in the area had inspired a $10,000 contribution from Maine philanthropist John Storer, on the condition that the school be open to all regardless of sex, race, or religion. In December 1869, the federal government formally conveyed the Lockwood House and three former armory residences to the school's trustees, one of whom was Frederick Douglass.

By the end of the 19th century, the promise of freedom and equality for blacks had been buried by Jim Crow laws and legal segregation. To combat these injustices, Dr. W.E.B. Du Bois and other leading African Americans created the Niagara Movement, which held its second conference on the campus of Storer College in 1906. The Niagara Movement was a forerunner of the NAACP.

In 1954, legal segregation was finally ended by the landmark school desegregation decision handed down by the Supreme Court in *Brown v. The Board of Education*. A year later, Storer College closed its doors. Today the National Park Service continues the college's educational mission by using part of the old campus as a training facility.

Harpers Ferry, ca. 1882.

Independence National Historical Park

143 South Third Street
Philadelphia, Pennsylvania 19106
215-965-2305
www.nps.gov/inde

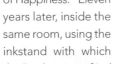

In 1776, atop the Pennsylvania State House, today known as Independence Hall, the State House Bell emblazoned with "Proclaim LIBERTY throughout all the Land, unto all the Inhabitants thereof," rang in the founding of a new nation. This new nation was founded on the ideals that "all men are created equal...endowed by their Creator" with the "unalienable rights of Life, Liberty, and the pursuit of Happiness." Eleven years later, inside the same room, using the inkstand with which the Declaration of Independence was signed, the U.S. Constitution was signed protecting the institution of slavery. In Congress Hall, a few yards away from the State House, the U.S. Congress passed the Fugitive Slave Act strengthening the Fugitive Slave Clause of the Constitution.

Independence Hall

Assembly Room

Eventually, the Declaration's ideas of liberty and equality would triumph. Three years after President Washington signed the Fugitive Slave Act into law, one of Washington's nine enslaved household laborers escaped using the Underground Railroad. Abolitionists locally and nationally protested the fugitive slave trials taking place inside Independence Hall using the State House Bell, renamed "The Liberty Bell," as their symbol and tirelessly worked to bring the ideals of the Declaration to fruition.

Independence National Historical Park preserves the buildings, stories, and memory of the people who struggled and continue to struggle to create a nation based on liberty and equality.

39

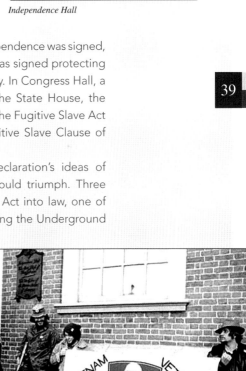

Vietnam Veterans exercising First Amendment right to protest.

Jamestown National Historic Site

Colonial National Historical Park
Yorktown, Virginia 23690
757-856-1200
www.nps.gov/jame

POWHATAN
Held this state & fashion when Capt. Smith was delivered to him prisoner 1607

Algonquin Chief Powhatan

Today, America is known as a melting pot of peoples and cultures. It all began in the early 17th century in Virginia with the coming together of people from three continents: the American Indians, the English, and the Africans. America's history actually began with the American Indians. However, as they left no written record of their culture, there is only archeology to tell us of this culture. Despite the English colonists' early struggles to survive in Virginia, the 1607 settlement evolved into a prosperous colony. As the colony expanded, the Virginia Indians were pushed out of their homeland. Then, in 1619, arrival of the Africans was recorded, marking the origin of slavery in English North America.

Historic Jamestowne is a unit within the larger Colonial National Historical Park and is the site of the first permanent English settlement in North America. Visit the park, walk in the steps of Captain John Smith and Pocahontas, and watch reenactors' demonstrations, to learn how the development of North America came about. Although there were other European settlements in America before Jamestown, our language and most of our customs and laws come from our English ancestry. Jamestown is the beginning of America.

A recreation of the James Fort of 1607.

Jefferson National Expansion Memorial

11 North 4th Street
St. Louis, Missouri 63102
314-655-1700
www.nps.gov/jeff

The interpretation of African American heritage at Jefferson National Expansion Memorial takes place in the Museum of Westward Expansion beneath the Gateway Arch, in exhibits viewed during the top of the arch tour, and at the historic Old Courthouse. In the museum, the stories of African American explorers, mountain men, soldiers, cowboys, and pioneer settlers are told through photographs and ranger programs.

One of the park's most famous stories is that of Dred Scott and his wife, Harriet, and their struggles to obtain freedom through the court system from 1846 to 1857. The case they launched in St. Louis's Old Courthouse led to an infamous Supreme Court decision that affected the entire nation and hastened the start of the Civil War.

A film shown in the Old Courthouse gives visitors a sense of the era and the courage of the Scotts and provides background information on urban slavery and ways in which African Americans used the court system to try to gain freedom. The building has two restored courtrooms that set the scene of the trials.

41

Gateway Arch framing the Old Courthouse.

Little Bighorn Battlefield National Monument

Exit 510 off I-90 Highway 212
Crow Agency, Montana 59022
406-638-2621
www.nps.gov/libi

Chief Sitting Bull

The Battle of Little Bighorn was fought along the ridges, steep bluffs, and ravines of the Little Bighorn River in South Central Montana on June 25 and 26, 1876. This site memorializes one of the Indians last armed efforts to preserve their way of life. As a result of the battle, 263 soldiers, including Lt. Col. George A. Custer and attached personnel of the U.S. Army's 7th Cavalry, died fighting several thousand Lakota Sioux, Northern Cheyenne, and some Arapaho warriors.

The Battle of Little Bighorn has come to symbolize the clash of two vastly different cultures: the buffalo/horse culture of the Northern Plains tribes and the highly industrial/agricultural-based culture of the United States, which was advancing primarily from the East Coast. This battle was not an isolated soldier versus warrior confrontation, but part of a much larger strategic campaign designed to force the capitulation of the nonreservation Sioux and Cheyenne.

The first part of the battle was a momentary victory for the Sioux and Cheyenne. Later, Gen. Philip Sheridan had the leverage to put more troops in the field. Lakota Sioux hunting grounds were invaded by powerful army expeditionary forces determined to confine the Sioux and Cheyenne to reservations. Most of the de-

Custer National Cemetery

clared "hostiles" had surrendered within one year of the fight, and the Black Hills were taken by the United States without compensation to the Indians.

Headstones at the battle site.

Little Rock Central High School National Historic Site

2120 Daisy L. Gatson Bates Drive
Little Rock, Arkansas 72202
501-374-1957
www.nps.gov/chsc

Inside foyer of Little Rock Central High School.

On May 17, 1954, the Supreme Court of the United States ruled in *Brown v. Board of Education of Topeka* that segregation in the public schools of the nation was unconstitutional. One of the first big tests of that decision came at Little Rock Central High School. On September 23, 1957, nine African Americans attempted to enroll in the formerly all-white school. Arkansas Governor Orville Faubus called in the National Guard to "prevent violence" and to keep the students from entering. After a federal judge forced Faubus to remove the troops, the Little Rock police were unable to control the crowd, and violence erupted. To enforce federal law, President Dwight D. Eisenhower sent the 101st Airborne Division to protect the students who entered the school and began attending classes. Tension remained at the school for some time, but an important first step in school integration had been taken.

Little Rock Central High School is an operating public school and is not open for visitors to tour on their own. Ranger-guided tours are limited to groups of 10 or fewer, and reservations must be made two weeks in advance. The best place to begin your visit is the park visitor center across from the school. Exhibits tell the story of those times, and interactive oral history stations give you a chance to hear the people who were there tell the story in their own words.

Little Rock Central High School

Maggie L. Walker
National Historic Site

600 North 2nd Street
Richmond, Virginia 23223
804-771-2017
www.nps.gov/mawa

Maggie L. Walker

In spite of humble beginnings in post-Civil War Richmond, Virginia, Maggie Lena Walker achieved national prominence as a businesswoman and community leader. Her business acumen, personality, and lifelong commitment to the Independent Order of St. Luke, a fraternal beneficial society that promoted humanitarian causes, fueled her climb to success. Through sound fiscal policies, a genius for public relations, and enormous energy, she took that dying organization and helped it thrive.

In 1903, Walker was the first African American woman in the United States to found a bank—The St. Luke Penny Savings Bank. That bank issued 625 mortgages to black families in its first years of operation, which was remarkable in a time when it was extremely difficult for African Americans to receive mortgages from other banks.

Walker devoted her life to civil rights advancement, economic empowerment, and educational opportunities for Jim Crow-era African Americans and for women. She served on the board of trustees for several women's groups, including the National Association of Colored Women and the Virginia Industrial School for Girls, as well as the Virginia Interracial Commission and the National Association for the Advancement of Colored People.

As newspaper editor, banker, and fraternal leader, Walker was an inspiration of pride and progress. Today, her home is preserved as a tribute to her vision, courage, and determination.

The National Park Service purchased Walker's house and its contents in 1979. The community where she resided exemplifies the success of African American entrepreneurship to this day.

Members of the Independent Order of St. Luke.

Manzanar National Historic Site

5001 Highway 395
Independence, California 93526
760-878-2194
www.nps.gov/manz

Schoolchildren at Manzanar.

Japan's attack on Pearl Harbor on December 7, 1941 led the United States into World War II and radically changed the lives of 120,000 men, women, and children of Japanese ancestry living in the United States. The attack intensified racial prejudices and led to fear of potential sabotage and espionage by Japanese American citizens and resident Japanese aliens.

In February 1942, President Franklin D. Roosevelt signed Executive Order 9066 authorizing the secretary of war to establish military areas, and to remove from those areas anyone who might threaten the war effort. Without due process, the government gave everyone of Japanese ancestry living on the West Coast only days to decide what to do with their houses, farms, businesses, and possessions. They did not know where they were going or for how long. Each family was assigned an identification number and loaded into cars, buses, trucks, and trains, taking only what they could carry. They were transported under military guard and interned at military-style camps in remote areas of Arizona, Arkansas, California, Colorado, Idaho, Oregon, Utah, Washington, and Wyoming.

Manzanar, located in the Owens Valley of California between the Sierra Nevada on the western side and the Inyo mountains on the eastern side, was typical of those camps. Manzanar National Historic Site was established to preserve the stories of those 120,000 Japanese Americans interned during World War II and to serve as a reminder to this and future generations of the fragility of American civil liberties.

Entrance to Manzanar.

Living quarters

Mount Williamson and cemetery monument.

Martin Luther King, Jr. Memorial

900 Ohio Drive, SW
Washington, DC 20024
202-426-6841
www.nps.gov/mlkm

August 28, 2011, the 48th anniversary of the groundbreaking March on Washington for Jobs and Freedom, witnessed the dedication of the Martin Luther King, Jr. Memorial. It is fitting that on that date, reminiscent of the defining moment in Dr. King's leadership in the civil rights movement, his legacy is further cemented into the tapestry of the American experience in the form of solid granite.

Dr. King became an important part of the African American struggle for freedom that began during the horrible era of slavery and continued throughout his life. He provided crucial leadership to African Americans who struggled for freedom in the deeply segregated Jim Crow South and throughout the rest of the United States. During his peaceful marches, he and his followers faced violence and the isolation of prison with a dignity that inspired many. He broke the bounds of intolerance, as he became a symbol recognized worldwide in the quest for civil rights for the citizens of the world.

The Martin Luther King, Jr. Memorial honors a man of conscience; the freedom movement of which he was a beacon; and his message of freedom, equality, justice, and love. It is the first memorial on the National Mall devoted, not to a president or war hero, but to a citizen activist for civil rights and peace, and it is tangible proof that Dr. King's dream lives on.

Martin Luther King, Jr. National Historic Site

450 Auburn Avenue, NE
Atlanta, Georgia 30312
404-331-5190
www.nps.gov/malu

Martin Luther King, Jr. is honored throughout the United States and the world for his leadership in the struggle for equality and human rights, his philosophy of nonviolent social change, and his work to promote world peace and economic equality. Beginning with the 1955 bus boycott in Alabama and ending with his assassination on April 4, 1968, Dr. King led the modern American civil rights movement for which he received the Nobel Peace Prize. His widow, Mrs. Coretta Scott King, acted upon her vision to preserve the works and ideals of her husband. In June 1968, she founded and was the first president of the Martin Luther King, Jr. Center for Nonviolent Social Change. She later advocated for the establishment of the Martin Luther King, Jr. National Historic Site that was to become a unit of the National Park Service.

The park's mission is to preserve, protect, and interpret the place where Martin Luther King, Jr. was born on January 15, 1929 and where he lived, worked, worshipped, and is buried. The site's key destinations include The King Center and Freedom Hall, Heritage Sanctuary at Historic Ebenezer Baptist Church, the tombs of Dr. King and Mrs. Coretta Scott King, the Birth Home, Historic Fire Station No. 6, and the National Park Service Visitor Center. The park offers tours of Dr. King's Birth Home; tickets are free and available on a first-come, first-served basis on the day of the tour.

Visitor Center exhibits

Mary McLeod Bethune Council House National Historic Site

1318 Vermont Avenue, NW
Washington, DC 20005
202-673-2402
www.nps.gov/mamc

First headquarters of the National Council of Negro Women.

By her own words and example, Mary McLeod Bethune demonstrated the value of education, a philosophy of universal love, and the wise and consistent use of political power in striving for racial and gender equality. The 15th of 17 children of former slaves, Bethune grew up amidst poverty and the oppression of the Reconstruction South, yet she rose to prominence as an educator, presidential advisor, and political activist. Through her own schooling by missionaries in South Carolina, Bethune recognized the importance of education in the emerging struggle for civil rights.

In 1904, Bethune founded the Daytona Educational and Industrial School for Negro Girls in Daytona Beach, Florida, which later merged with the Cookman Institute to become Bethune-Cookman College. In 2007, the school became Bethune-Cookman University.

Bethune achieved her greatest recognition at the Washington, D.C., townhouse that is now the Mary McLeod Bethune Council House National Historic Site. The Council House was the first headquarters of the National Council of Negro Women (NCNW), established by Bethune in 1935, and was her last home in Washington, D.C. From here, she and the NCNW spearheaded strategies and developed programs that advanced the interests of African American women. The site commemorates Bethune's leadership in the black women's rights movement from 1943 to 1949, and she continued to be an important voice for human rights until her death in 1955 at the age of 79.

Mary McLeod Bethune Memorial

Minidoka National Historic Site

221 North State Street
Hagerman, Idaho 83332
208-933-4100
www.nps.gov/miin

The Japanese on the West Coast of the United States had made lives for themselves in spite of discrimination, but on December 7, 1941, everything changed. After the attack on Pearl Harbor, panicked people believed every Japanese person could be a potential spy, ready to assist in an invasion that was expected at any moment. Many people came to believe that everyone of Japanese ancestry, including American citizens, needed to be removed from the West Coast.

In February 1942, President Franklin D. Roosevelt signed an executive order that moved nearly 120,000 Japanese and Japanese Americans into isolated relocation centers in Arizona, Arkansas, California, Colorado, Idaho, Oregon, Utah, Washington, and Wyoming. The temporary, tarpaper-covered barracks, the guard towers, and most of the barbed-wire fences are gone now, but the people who spent years of their lives in the centers will never forget them.

In 1979, Minidoka Relocation Center was added to the National Register of Historic Places, and in 2001, it became the 385th unit of the National Park Service. Today, there is a small gravel parking area, paths, and interpretative signs about the internment located at the stone guardhouse and waiting room beyond the Hunt Bridge. Also commemorated here are the Japanese Americans from the relocation center who died serving in the military during World War II. Nearly 1,000 people from Minidoka served in the army, and Minidoka had the largest casualty list of the 10 relocation centers.

Tarpaper-covered barracks

Natchez National Historical Park

1 Melrose Montebello Parkway
Natchez, Mississippi 39120
601-446-5790
www.nps.gov/natc

Melrose Estate today.

Natchez National Historical Park interprets the lives of slaves through guided walks of the slave quarters, mansions, and grounds at Melrose. An excellent example of a planter's home, Melrose has one of the few intact and original slave quarters, with exhibits and interpretive panels that depict the lives of the residents.

The William Johnson House interprets the life of William Johnson. Known as the "Barber of Natchez," Johnson began his life as a slave. His owner, who was probably his father, freed him at age 11. Johnson bought a barbershop in 1830 from his brother-in-law and taught the trade to free black boys. Shortly after establishing the barbershop in downtown Natchez, he began to keep a diary. The diary, found inside the attic in his home, chronicled his life as a freed man. Although an African American, Johnson owned 15 slaves at the time of his death. His diaries do not reflect his feelings about slavery or race. However, Johnson often wrote about Steven, one of his slaves who caused him strife and grief. Johnson's 16 years' worth of diaries detailing his business activities and local news provide the best autobiographical account of a free black man in the Deep South before the Civil War and one of the best sources of information on daily life in antebellum Natchez.

National Underground Railroad Network to Freedom

www.nps.gov/ugrr

The Underground Railroad—the resistance to enslavement through escape and flight through the end of the Civil War—refers to the efforts of enslaved African Americans to gain their freedom by escaping bondage. Wherever slavery existed, there were efforts to escape, at first to communities in rugged terrain away from settled areas, and later across state and international borders. While most of the enslaved began and completed their journeys unassisted, each subsequent decade in which slavery was legal in the United States saw an increase in active efforts to assist escape.

The decision to assist a freedom seeker may have been spontaneous. However, in some places, and particularly after the Fugitive Slave Act of 1850, the Underground Railroad was deliberate and organized.

The National Underground Railroad Network to Freedom commemorates the stories of the men and women who risked everything for freedom and those who helped them. The Network to Freedom, through shared leadership with local, state, and federal entities as well as interested individuals and organizations, promotes programs and partnerships to commemorate the historical significance of the Underground Railroad and to educate the public.

The Underground Railroad extended through the Civil War as thousands of enslaved African Americans used the opportunity of approaching Union forces to escape and seek protection in contraband camps. Many of the men subsequently enlisted in the U.S. Colored Troops and served as soldiers or sailors during the war. A number of Network to Freedom sites recognize this history.

Freedmen's Monument at Fort Raleigh NHS.

Breaking the shackles.

Nicodemus National Historic Site

304 Washington Avenue
Nicodemus, Kansas 67625
785-839-4233
www.nps.gov/nico

Nicodemus–one of the oldest Black towns on the Western Plains.

Some former slaves did not accept life after Reconstruction in the South. They left the plantations and traveled north looking for new opportunities. They were called Exodusters, and most headed to Kansas, in part because they knew this was where John Brown fought against slavery. Nicodemus represents the involvement of those African Americans in the western expansion and settlement of the Great Plains. The oldest and only remaining all-black town west of the Mississippi River, at its height Nicodemus included about 700 people living in the town and township.

Nicodemus is a symbolic name associated with the biblical personality with whom Jesus talked about being born again. In 1864, American composer Henry Clay Work published a popular slave-era song called "Wake Nicodemus." Later, his song was slightly modified and used to promote the settlement of Nicodemus. Farming was the main industry, and corn and wheat were the main crops. There were also several businesses including, general stores, grocery stores, hotels, pharmacies, millinery shops, barbershops, and a bank.

Eleven people are now living in Nicodemus. Ten are descendants of the original settlers. Three descendants live in the township north of town. The number of people living in the town changes frequently and includes absentee black farmers and just one black farmer still living on the original family land.

Port Chicago Naval Magazine National Memorial

c/o John Muir National Historic Site
4202 Alhambra Avenue
Martinez, California 94553
925-228-8860
www.nps.gov/poch

In the segregated military of 1944, many African Americans worked as stevedores, loading and unloading ships. At Port Chicago, they received little or no training and were told the munitions they were loading were not active. Then, on the evening of July 17, 1944, a massive explosion lit up the night sky. Two ships being loaded with ammunition for the Pacific Theater troops blew up. Of the 320 men killed instantly, 202 were African American.

Site of the tragic WWII homeland disaster.

Less than a month after the explosion, 328 survivors, including more than 300 African Americans, were transferred to other facilities. They were ordered onto the loading pier of the Mare Island naval facility, a few miles away from Port Chicago. Most of the black sailors refused the order because of the possibility of another explosion. Of those, 250 were arrested and charged with mutiny. Reluctantly, 200 of them returned to duty. The remaining 50 sailors who still refused to load munitions were found guilty of mutiny, sentenced to prison, and received dishonorable discharges.

The tragedies of the explosion and the courts-martial of African American sailors illustrated the racial discrimination in the military at that time. After the war, in January 1946, those men were released from prison, granted clemency, and finished the remaining months of their enlistment in the Pacific.

In June 1945, the navy began desegregating its units. Then, in 1948, President Harry S Truman signed Executive Order 9981 desegregating the armed forces.

Port Chicago, a touchstone for desegregation of the military.

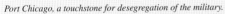

53

Sand Creek Massacre National Historic Site

55411 County Road W
Eads, Colorado 81036
719-438-5916
www.nps.gov/sand

Sand Creek Massacre survivors.

By 1864, a combination of cultural demands on the Plains environment and natural factors caused food and fuel to become increasingly scarce. Traditional campsites used by the Cheyenne and Arapaho along rivers and streams were unable to support winter encampments. In the fall of 1864, Black Kettle, White Antelope, and other Cheyenne chiefs established a winter campsite near the south bend of Big Sandy Creek. Well over 100 tepees dotted the valley while hundreds of horses grazed nearby.

Wayside depicting the attack.

Earlier that fall, a large group of Arapaho and some Cheyenne had camped near Fort Lyon. The Fort Lyon reserve was also the site of the Upper Arkansas Indian Agency. In November, after a change in orders and change in commanders at Fort Lyon, the tribes were prohibited from camping near the fort. Nearly all the Cheyenne and a small camp of Arapaho moved to Sand Creek. On November 29, 1864, U.S. soldiers attacked this peaceful encampment of over 500 people. More than 150 Indians were killed; most were women, children, or the elderly. Survivors of the attack fled to the North, hoping to reach a larger band of Cheyenne. The massacre profoundly influenced United States-Indian relations and the structure of the Cheyenne and Arapaho tribes.

Sand Creek battle ground monument.

Sand Creek Massacre National Historic Site was established in 2007 to preserve and protect the cultural and natural landscape and to enhance the public's understanding of this tragedy.

Blankets, hides, and other offerings at massacre overlook.

Selma to Montgomery National Historic Trail

2 Broad Street
Selma, Alabama 36701
334-872-0509
www.nps.gov/semo

The Selma to Montgomery National Historic Trail was established by Congress in 1996 to commemorate the events, people, and route of the 1965 Voting Rights March in Alabama. The route is also designated as a National Scenic Byway/ All-American Road. Visitors are encouraged to drive the historic route from Selma to Montgomery, Alabama; view the significant sites along the 54-mile trail; and take part in the trail's year-round special events.

The Selma Interpretive Center opened its doors to the public in March 2011 and serves as the welcome center to the trail, located at the foot of the Edmund Pettus Bridge. The center offers a video, exhibits, and bookstore. In addition, it provides a breathtaking view of the Edmund Pettus Bridge, which is famously known as the site of "Bloody Sunday" and serves as the focus for Selma's annual Bridge Crossing Jubilee.

At the trail's midpoint in White Hall, Alabama, visitors to the Lowndes County Interpretive Center can learn the history of the Selma to Montgomery March by watching a 25-minute film inside the theater, and can connect to the stories and events through the museum exhibits, photographs, and an outdoor walking trail. Park rangers are available for orientations, talks, and tours. Groups and individuals are asked to make reservations before arrival, although walk-ins are always welcomed.

Martin Luther King, Jr., and Coretta Scott King (center) on the Selma to Montgomery march.

Statue of Liberty
National Monument

Liberty Island
New York, New York 10004
212-363-3200
www.nps.gov/stli

In 1886, the Statue of Liberty was built as a symbol of democratic government and enlightenment ideals, as well as a celebration of the Union's victory in the American Civil War and the abolition of slavery. Edouard de Laboulaye, the French political thinker, U.S. Constitution expert, and abolitionist was a firm supporter of President Abraham Lincoln and his fight for abolition.

After the abolition of slavery and the Union's victory in the Civil War in 1865, Laboulaye's wishes for freedom and democracy were turning into a reality in the United States. To honor these achievements, Laboulaye proposed that a gift be created for the United States on behalf of France. Laboulaye hoped that by calling attention to the achievements of the United States, the French people would be inspired to call for their own democracy in the face of a repressive monarchy.

When the statue was completed, it not only represented democracy, but also symbolized American independence and the end of all types of servitude and oppression. A broken shackle and chain lie at the statue's right foot. The chain disappears beneath the draperies, only to reappear in front of her left foot, its end link broken. However, although the broken shackle is a powerful image, the meaning behind it was not yet a reality for African Americans in 1886 and would not be a reality for at least another one hundred years.

Immigrants arrive at the "land of liberty."

Trail of Tears
National Historic Trail

1100 Old Santa Fe Trail
Santa Fe, New Mexico 87505
505-988-6098
www.nps.gov/trte

In 1838, the U.S. government forcibly removed more than 16,000 Cherokee Indian people from their homelands in Alabama, Georgia, North Carolina, and Tennessee and sent them to Indian Territory (today known as Oklahoma). The impact to the Cherokee was devastating. Hundreds of Cherokee died during their trip west, and thousands more perished from the consequences of relocation. This tragic chapter in American and Cherokee history became known as the Trail of Tears and culminated in the implementation of the Indian Removal Act of 1830, which mandated the removal of all American Indian tribes east of the Mississippi River to lands in the West.

The Trail of Tears National Historic Trail commemorates the removal of the Cherokee and the paths that 17 Cherokee detachments followed westward. Today, the trail encompasses about 2,200 miles of land and water routes and traverses portions of nine states.

The National Park Service, in partnership with other federal agencies, state and local agencies, non-profit organizations, and private landowners, administers the Trail of Tears National Historic Trail. Participating national historic trail sites display the official trail logo. The trail passes through the present-day states of Alabama, Arkansas, Georgia, Illinois, Kentucky, Missouri, North Carolina, Oklahoma, and Tennessee. Due to the trail's length, you may decide to travel its entirety or just visit a few sites.

Cherokee leader John Ross fought Indian removal policies.

Montage depicting the Trail of Tears.

Tuskegee Airmen National Historic Site

16116 Chappie James Avenue
Tuskegee Institute, Alabama 36087
334-724-0922
www.nps.gov/tuai

In spite of adversity and limited opportunities, African Americans played a significant role in U.S. military history over the past 300 years. They were denied military leadership roles and skilled training because many people believed they lacked qualifications for combat duty. Before 1940, they were barred from flying for the U.S. military. Civil rights organizations and the black press exerted pressure that resulted in the formation of an African American squadron based in Tuskegee, Alabama, in 1941. They became known as the Tuskegee Airmen.

African American pilots at Moton Field.

"Tuskegee Airmen" refers to all who were involved in the so-called "Tuskegee Experiment" —the U.S. Army Air Corps program to train African Americans to fly and maintain combat aircraft. They included pilots, navigators, bombardiers, maintenance and support staff, instructors, and all personnel who kept the planes in the air.

The military selected Tuskegee Institute to train pilots because of its commitment to aeronautical training. The institute had the facilities and engineering and technical instructors, as well as a climate for year-round flying. The first Civilian Pilot Training Program students completed their instruction in May 1940. The Tuskegee program was then expanded and became the center for African American aviation during World War II.

The Tuskegee Airmen overcame segregation and prejudice to become one of the most highly respected fighter groups of World War II. They proved conclusively that African Americans could fly and maintain sophisticated combat aircraft. Their achievements, together with the men and women who supported them, paved the way for full integration of the U.S. military.

Women's Rights National Historical Park

136 Fall Street
Seneca Falls, New York 13148
315-568-2991
www.nps.gov/wori

Statues of the first wave of women's rights activists.

The women's rights movement was the offspring of abolition. Many people actively supported both reforms. Several participants in the 1848 first Woman's Rights Convention in Seneca Falls, New York, had already labored in the antislavery movement. The organizers and their families—the Motts, Wrights, Stantons, M'Clintocks, and Hunts—were active abolitionists to a greater or lesser degree. Frederick Douglass, noted abolitionist and former slave, attended and addressed the 1848 convention.

Arguments for women's rights came from experiences in the antislavery movement. As reformers, women developed organizational skills necessary for a successful social movement. They learned to write persuasively, raise funds, organize supporters and events, and speak to large groups of men and women about important political and social issues. In the service of antislavery, women found their voices.

At the 1848 first Woman's Rights Convention, the Declaration of Sentiments, drafted by Elizabeth Cady Stanton and Elizabeth and Mary Ann M'Clintock, was read and signed by 100 men and women. Claiming "that all men and women are created equal," the signers called for extending to women the right to vote, control property, sign legal documents, serve on juries, and enjoy equal access to education and the professions.

Today at Women's Rights National Historical Park, the connection between the organizers of the 1848 convention and the antislavery movement is incorporated into interpretive programs. The M'Clintock House, a site on the Underground Railroad in nearby Waterloo, offers a unique opportunity to learn about the relationship between these two reform movements of the 19th century.

Wesleyan Chapel, site of the first Woman's Rights Convention.

Back cover: Missouri Governor Frederick Gardner signing the
resolution ratifying the 19th constitutional amendment, 1919.

Special thanks to NPS Chief Historian Robert K. Sutton,
NPS Interpretive Specialist Doeun "Duey" Kol,
and Blake Bell at Homestead NM of America.

Thanks to the Estate of Dr. Martin Luther King, Jr. and
Intellectual Properties Management, Atlanta, Georgia.
The name, likeness, and quotations of Dr. Martin Luther King, Jr. are the
intellectual property of The Estate of Dr. Martin Luther King, Jr., Inc.
and are used with express permission.

Image sources
The Granger Collection, New York: page 3, 4, 5, 6, 7, 8,
9, 10, 12, 15, 16, 18, 20, 21, 22 top, 23, 24 top,
back cover; Library of Congress: 24 bottom, 25, 32, 37, 45, 49, 57 top.
All other images courtesy of the National Park Sevice.

For more information on the national parks visit www.nps.gov